A GREEN CHRISTMAS

A GREEN CHRISTMAS

AN ENVIRONMENTAL MUSICAL FOR JUNIOR & MIDDLE SCHOOLS
Dave Ramell Sturgess

For my parents

Acknowledgements
My thanks to:
Pamela Wallace – for writing from my singing
Brian Wallace – for making connections
Deidre Richards – for reading my writing!
Ken Abel – for invaluable advice
Sue – for all her help and support

A GREEN CHRISTMAS was first performed at Tunstead Primary School,
Tunstead, Nr. Wroxham, Norfolk, Christmas 1989.

Note to Producer:

A licence is required to perform this work. Please address your application to Education Dept., International Music Publications, Woodford Trading Estate, Southend Road, Woodford Green, Essex IG8 8HN, stating the title of the work and the proposed dates of performance.

Duration: approximately 60 minutes
Piano arrangements and text editing by Barrie Carson Turner

First Published 1991
© International Music Publications
Southend Road, Woodford Green,
Essex IG8 8HN, England.

215-2-648

NOTES ON PERFORMANCE

STAGING

The staging should be planned around two basic sets: the forest (scenes) and the cave (scenes). The latter may also be used for the Squirts and Marge & Dot, scenes 4 & 5.

For the forest scenes, a backdrop of brown Christmas trees line a central track which disappears into the distance. This backdrop may remain in position throughout, although a curtain drawn across it, or black drape lowered in front of it for the cave and house interior scenes would be preferable. Free-standing large rocks or rock panels may be placed towards the back of the stage during the cave scenes. If it is not covered in any other way, then several large rock panels will hide the forest backdrop. If rock panels are used, the reverse side may be painted to look like house interiors for scenes 4 & 5.

The forest scenery may be considerably enhanced by making free-standing Christmas tree panels, with brown trees painted on one side and green trees on the other (brown trees for Scenes 1, 3, 6, 7 & 8; green trees for Scene 12).

The traffic lights can be easily made from a strong cardboard box mounted on a sturdy carpet roll tube which is supported on a wooden base. Car headlamp bulbs make an ideal light source. These can be mounted on small tin foil pie dishes; they act as ideal reflectors. Coloured filters or translucent coloured paper should be mounted a safe distance from the bulbs.

The signpost may be a simple wooden construction with the two pointers set at right angles. One arm points to Disaster and Destruction (down the track on the backdrop). The other arm points to Green World. The traffic lights and the signpost should be positioned either side of the track and towards the back of the stage.

Scenes 4 and 5 need two chairs and a small table. The scene with the Squirts also requires an artificial Christmas tree. The construction of a humanoid robot makes an excellent design and technology project. The robot may be anything from a simple junk model to a complex creation with built-in loudspeaker, flashing lights, rotating antennas, etc. The robot should be as large and imposing as possible but at the same time relatively easy to move on and off stage during the blackouts. It should be positioned centre stage, towards the back when addressing the Grey Gang.

The explosion in the scene Grey Failure can be created using sound effects and flashing lights. For the more ambitious, pieces can be made to fall off the robot and smoke effects used.

The green star may be an illuminated suspension or a projected image.

A suspended planet Earth, with a sad face drawn over a simple map on one side and a smiling face on the reverse, can easily be made and supported inside a large plastic hula-hoop. The Earth's sad face can remain suspended above the stage until the final scene when it is turned round to show the smiling side, complete with suitable illumination, e.g. spotlight, plus edging of Christmas tree lights. During the singing of *A Green Christmas*, the Narrator, Grey Gang and the performer who plays the voice of 'Disaster' enter and join in with the singing.

COSTUMES

These may be simple green or grey clothes for the gang members. The rest of the cast may wear ordinary clothing. The effectiveness of the costumes, however, will be much greater if the Green Gang wear a green uniform, with the Green hand sign displayed prominently on their clothes, and the Grey Gang wear costumes that depict their character, e.g. Dr Fluorocarbon dressed as an aerosol can; Nite and Phos as fertilizer sacks; Major Threat in military uniform. The performer playing the voice of

Disaster should if possible be dressed in a metallic costume, with the word "Disaster" incorporated into the design (in this way the performer will be recognizable in the finale scene).

LIGHTING

The forest scenes should be brightly lit, with the exception of the scene with the Litter family, during which the lighting gradually fades. Scenes 4 & 5 also require bright lighting, although a warmer tinge should be used for these two interior scenes.

The robot and the traffic lights both need an off-stage switching system. Flashing lights are required during the explosion of the robot. For the cave scenes, cold blue lighting is recommended. This may also be used for Con's nightmare, although a spotlight would be preferable.

SOUND

An echo unit and/or a voice synthesizer are preferable for the robot's voice. These can also be used to create the sound of an explosion if you are unable to obtain a tape or do not have access to a synthesizer keyboard with an appropriate effect.

In addition to the use of a piano and/or electronic keyboard, the song *A.C.I.D. R.A.I.N.* lends itself to the guitar. The song *Grey Matter,* with its strong rock beat, would benefit from the use of a drum.

PROPS

The following props are essential, although additional props may also be used to enhance the production.
A green folder for the Narrator's text
Scene 1 – Traffic lights and signpost; photo fit picture of Major Threat
Scene 3 – Wrist watch
Scene 4 – 4 aerosol cans (empty), artificial Christmas tree, safety razor, small table, 2 - 4 chairs, card for
             Dr Fluorocarbon
Scene 5 – Small table, 2 chairs, 2 cups and saucers
Scene 6 – Giant-size book of blue litmus paper with one detachable leaf that is blue on one side and red on the other
Scene 7 – Picnic basket containing: paper plates, plastic cups, wrapped sweets, drink cans, artificial food, table cloth
Scene 10 – Newspaper
Scene 12 – Traffic lights and signpost, two letters in envelopes

ACTIONS TO SONGS

WHAT'S ALL THIS THEN?	The police officers bend their knees.
GREY MATTER	Hands over hearts when the word *hearts* is sung.
	Finger pointing to side of head when the word *brain* is sung.
STOP, DON'T SHOOT	The Green Gang point to the Squirts as the words of the song ask, "Did you look? Have you checked? What did it say?"
SMILING WORLD	The Green Gang point to the world's face which is suspended and illuminated above the stage.

Note: P.S.T. is pronounced *psst!*

MUSICAL NUMBERS

CAST

(Male and female parts have been indicated where it is not obvious from the character name.)

GREEN GANG

Con Servation *(f)*

*Ozone Friendly *(m)*

Sus Stainable *(m)*

**Rene Newable

Rees Cycle

P. H. Neutral *(m)*

Rube Ishbin

Lorraine Forest

POLICE

Sgt. Pratt

WPC Bolder

PC Stone

GREY GANG

Disaster *(off-stage voice only – m/f)*

Major Threat

Miss Guided

Miss Lead

Dr. C. Fluorocarbon *(f)*

A.Sid Rain

Chuck Itaway

Nite Rates *(m)*

Phos Phates *(m)*

Green House *(f)*

C.O. Two *(f)*

Ray D. Ation

Dee Forestation

Sue Age

SQUIRTS

Mr Sid Squirt

Mrs Sandra Squirt

Sharon Squirt

Sean Squirt

OTHERS

Narrator *(m/f)*

Marge

Dot

Teeny, Weeny Greens *(any number)*

LITTERS

Mr Les Litter

Mrs Lil Litter

Lucy Litter

Linda Litter

Laurie Litter

Lennie Litter

OFF-STAGE CHOIR *(any number)*

*Ozone's abbreviation 'Oz' is pronounced *Ohze.*

**Pronounced *Rean.*

1. OVERTURE

9

10

2. WHAT'S ALL THIS, THEN?

CUE: PC STONE: . . . Pretty grotty I'd say.

3. GREY MATTER

CUE: DISASTER: Get Rich Everyone. Yes! *(Evil, hysterical laughter)*

4. DARK DAYS

CUE: NARRATOR: She falls asleep and has a strange dream. *Exit* NARRATOR.

5. STOP, DON'T SHOOT

CUE: OZ: May we have a look at these cans please? *(They walk round inspecting the cans.)* I thought so!

22

Did you look? Have you checked? What does it say?——— Did you look? Have you checked?

What does it say? ——— Please make sure that you read what it says Be-

fore you de-cide to buy it. Chlor-o - fluor-o - car-bons can do

lots of—— harm And no one should de - ny it.

6. A.C.I.D. R.A.I.N.

CUE: *Lights up. Enter* P.H. *and* RENE.

7. WE ARE THE TEENY, WEENY GREENS

CUE: RENE: Yes, you can start by cheering up P.H.!

28

8. LITTER LOUT ROCK

CUE: *Lights up. The* LITTER FAMILY *arrive with their picnic basket.*

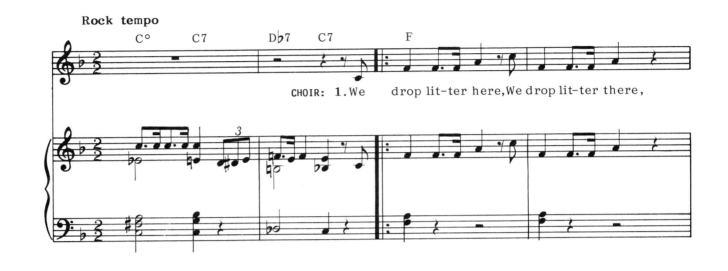

CHOIR: 1. We drop lit-ter here, We drop lit-ter there,

We drop lit-ter ev-e-ry-where.— We drop it on the pave-ment,
We drop it by the road-side, In
We drop it in our play-grounds,

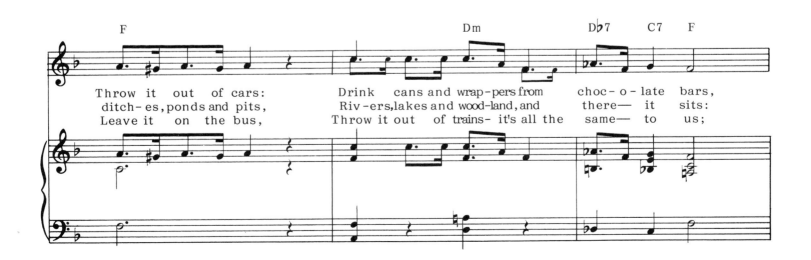

Throw it out of cars: Drink cans and wrap-pers from choc-o-late bars,
ditch-es, ponds and pits, Riv-ers, lakes and wood-land, and there— it sits:
Leave it on the bus, Throw it out of trains- it's all the same— to us;

31

9. SMILING WORLD

CUE: CON: Come on everyone. Come on Sergeant. Green world here we come!

10. A GREEN CHRISTMAS

CUE: ALL: Happy Christmas!